By the Numbers

Books by James Richardson

By the Numbers

Interglacial: New and Selected Poems & Aphorisms

Vectors: Aphorisms and Ten-Second Essays

How Things Are

A Suite for Lucretians

As If

Vanishing Lives: Tennyson, D.G. Rossetti, Swinburne and Yeats

Second Guesses

Thomas Hardy: The Poetry of Necessity

Reservations

James Richardson By the Numbers

COPPER CANYON PRESS
PORT TOWNSEND, WASHINGTON

Cover art: John Schaefer, *Sun Surf,* 2009. Oil on canvas,
12 x 12 inches.

Copper Canyon Press is in residence at Fort Worden State Park in Port
Townsend, Washington, under the auspices of Centrum. Centrum is a
gathering place for artists and creative thinkers from around the world,
students of all ages and backgrounds, and audiences seeking extraordi-
nary cultural enrichment.

LIBRARY OF CONGRESS CATALOGING-IN-PUBLICATION DATA
Richardson, James, 1950–
By the numbers / James Richardson.
    p. cm.
ISBN 978-1-55659-320-8
I. Title.

PS3568.I3178B9 2010
811'.54—dc22

                                    2010019847

98765432 first printing

COPPER CANYON PRESS
Post Office Box 271
Port Townsend, Washington 98368
www.coppercanyonpress.org

Acknowledgments

Thanks to the editors who first gave some of these poems a place:

Alhambra Poetry Calendar 2010: "Roads Not Taken"
Connotation Press: An Online Artifact: "Origin of Language,"
  "Shore Town, Winter"
Fulcrum: "Iron Age," "Pygmalion among the Young,"
  "Twilight of a God"
Gulf Coast: "Red, Green, Blue," "Room Temperature," "To a
  Tea"
The Literary Review: "The Stars in Order Of"
Narrative: "Are We Alone? *or* Physics You Can Do at Home,"
  "Bit Parts," "Echo"
Painted Bride Quarterly: "Roads Taken"
Pleiades: "Apollo at Happy Hour," "Apollo in Age," "Black-
  out," "By the Numbers," "Head-On," "Orpheus at Last
  Call," "Ovidian Deposition," "Songs for Senility,"
  "Twilight of a God"
Redivider: "The Rich Man Sotto Voce," "Star"
Smartish Pace: "Emergency Measures"
Yale Review: "The God Who," "Postmortem Georgic,"
  "Special Victims Unit"

"End of Summer," "In Shakespeare," and "Subject, Verb,
  Object" originally appeared in *The New Yorker*. "Subject,
  Verb, Object" was reprinted in *The Best American Poetry
  2009*. "End of Summer" was reprinted in *Alhambra
  Poetry Calendar 2009*.

"Metallurgy for Dummies" and "State-Sponsored" were first
  published in *Tin House*. "Metallurgy for Dummies" was
  reprinted in *Pushcart Prize XXXIV: Best of the Small
  Presses* (2010).

"Northwest Passage" won the 2007 The Writer Magazine/ Emily Dickinson Award of the Poetry Society of America and was first printed in the program of its annual awards ceremony.

Selections from "Vectors 3.0: Even More Aphorisms and Ten-Second Essays" have appeared in *The Bloomsbury Review, Hamilton Stone Review,* and *The Literary Review.* "Vectors 2.3: 50 Aphorisms and Ten-Second Essays," first published in *The American Poetry Review,* was reprinted in *The Best American Poetry 2010.*

Thanks to Paul Muldoon and David Orr for taking a look at a draft.

And more than thanks to my best Poetry People, Connie Hassett and Cat Richardson.

BBR 1923–2008

JER 1923–2008

CONTENTS

By the Numbers

I. Bit Parts

Northwest Passage

That faint line in the dark
might be the shore
of some heretofore unknown
small hour.

This fir-scent on the wind
must be the forests
of the unheardof month
between July and August.

In Shakespeare

In Shakespeare a lover turns into an ass
as you would expect. Others confuse
their consciences with ghosts and witches.
Old men throw everything away
when they panic and can't feel their lives.
They pinch themselves, pierce themselves with twigs,
cliffs, lightning, to die—yes, finally—in glad pain.

You marry a woman you've never talked to,
a woman you thought was a boy.
Sixteen years go by as a curtain billows
once, twice. Your children are lost,
they come back, you don't remember how.
A love turns to a statue in a dress, the statue
comes back to life, O god, it's all so realistic
I can't stand it. *Whereat I weep and sing.*

Such a relief to burst from the theater
into our cool, imaginary streets
where we know who's who and what's what,
and command with MetroCards our destinations.
Where no one with a story struggling in him
convulses as it eats its way out,
and no one in an antiseptic corridor
or in deserts or in downtown darkling plains
staggers through an Act that just will not end,
eyes burning with the burning of the dead.

Special Victims Unit

Actually Persephone loved his loving her,
dark-browed, so serious: it proved something about her.
And for him, gloomy, overwhelmed with himself,
her brightness was more beautiful than beauty
and he basked in it. But when his turn came to shine back
it seemed her feelings were a storm of flowers
he could not gather, and the story gets ordinary:
he is angry at his heart and hurts her.

Demeter gets confused. Did a god steal her daughter,
or has she been living all this time in Manhattan
with her difficult husband, difficult job, difficult cat
and visiting once a year? Her love for what is lost
spreads so thinly over the planet
it's not love anymore but weather. She goes to the police:
Benson and Stabler find her story dubious.

More so when they learn she never had a daughter,
though she was one, and that her vaunted power over harvests
apparently doesn't extend to her wilting houseplants.
As for those Hellish threats on her machine?
Phone records show that dark voice was her own.
Actually she has bipolar Multiple Personality Disorder,
solution to all plot dilemmas. Fair enough,
since cop shows can't say what we'd say: *Life is a dream,
and we are everyone we dream.*
                          When they come to get her,
her hands are clawed in the chainlink of the playground.
Hades, Demeter, Persephone form in her face of cloud.
She's watching, of course, two girls on swings,
one going up while the other goes down.

Subject, Verb, Object

I is not ego, not the sum
of your unique experiences,
just, democratically,
whoever's talking,
a kind of motel room,
yours till the end—
that is, of the sentence.

The language, actually,
doesn't think *I*'s important,
stressing, even in
grandiose utterance—
e.g., I *came*
I *saw* I *conquered*—
the other syllables.

Oh, it's a technical problem,
sure, the rhyme
on oh-so-open
lie, cry, I,
harder to stitch tight
than the ozone
hole in the sky.

But worst is its plodding insistence—
I, I, I—
somebody huffing uphill,
face red as a Stop sign,
scared by a doctor
or some *He She It*
surprised in the mirror.

Emergency Measures

I take Saturday's unpopulated trains,
sitting at uncontagious distances,
change at junctions of low body count, in off-hours,
and on national holidays especially, shun stadia
and other zones of efficient kill ratio,
since there is no safety anymore in numbers.

I wear the dull colors of nesting birds,
invest modestly in diverse futures,
views and moods undiscovered by tourists,
buy nothing I can't carry or would need to sell,
and since I must rest, maintain at several addresses
hardened electronics and three months of water.

And it is thus I favor this unspecific café,
choose the bitterest roast, and only the first sip
of your story, sweet but so long, and poignantly limited
by appointments neither can be late for, and why now
I will swim through the crowd to the place it is flowing away from,
my concerned look and *Excuse me excuse me* suggesting
I am hurrying back for my umbrella or glasses
or some thrilling truth they have all completely missed.

Metallurgy for Dummies

Faint bronze of the air,
a bell I can't quite hear.

The sky they call gunmetal
over gunmetal reservoir,

the launch, aluminum,
cutting to the center,

waters bittered with the whisk
of aluminum propellers

(your gold drink stirred
with a gold forefinger).

*

Faint tinnitus,
where is it?

Air silver with a trillion
wireless calls,

stop-quick stop-quick
of sweep hands,

crickets and downed lines,
their sing of tension,

that out-of-earshot
too-bright CD sun,

the heads of presidents
sleet sleet in your jacket.

*

They were right,
those alchemists.
Anything—

tin-cold
eye of salamander,

a fly's
green shield and styli
on your wrist,

distinctly six—
anything might—

mutterings in the wet,
two-packs-a-day
brass of sax, bright

tears pestled,

or your hair's backlit
(same as the rain's)
slender metals—

anything might flash out...

*

Surely one sip,
mused Midas,
gin and silver,

surely her fine engine tuned
to a dial tone,

surely her famous sway,
gone Gold, gone Double Platinum,
Rare Earth, gone Transuranic...

*

Anything slow,
slash-black and copper
monarch settling,

the shy key's glint and turn,

sunny-cloudy
brass-and-tarnish fruit
paused at your lips, reflecting.

Any velocity,

water under the bridge
my leap
like dropped change rings on,

or seen from a train
chicory's blue
extrusion to a wire of blur,

the train itself
(of thought)
on its track and track and track,

your soft, incredible metals.

*

...surely these vast reserves
(Midas, that treasurer, surmised)
I must address

with a safecracker's
listening touch.

I'll be the anti-thief
slipping certificates of silver,
the slim faux-platinum

yen of credit,
palms flat,
over and over into her skintight pockets.

*

Eyes, blank or deep,
a lake
gone bright dark bright

(on thin ice giving way—

one: roll up the window
two: when the car fills...)

the fatal-in-seconds
keen cold of a mirror,

the blank bright blank

that any word might,
any word might not.

*

No one my touch
(that treasurer says)
can bear and tell

(apparently did not touch himself).

*

Wine so cold it's nails,
rings in the glass, poured,

your ring and its click
two-three, and click,
the bar awash

in digital and silver
whispers of the disc,

yes-no, yes
yes,
and This

Just In:
incredible metals

the shifting of your silks
imagines, unimagines,

the thought-blue
alloy of your lids,

the pistol
chill of your lips
my lips might freeze to.

Head-On

Flashing vehicles, unurgent lounging
tell you what it's too late for.
Don't rubberneck.
Don't look down the front of death's dress.
Don't say that white oblong on a gurney
looks like a bobsled, looks like room service.
Don't say it looks like a man,
all bright days jarred from his brain
like droplets from a branch.

Iron Age

Lest he could not make out my name tag,
I signed that I was a god, and would eat.
He brought me, as was meet, utensils,
but served, Lycaon, pans of scorn: sauté
of which of the human muscles I won't say.

No problem. Nothing I had not imagined
as vividly as its happening. Whereas a man
concocts strange sauces for his cruelty
that he may forget what meat he feasts on:
thinner and thinner his wife, his pale subjects,
his guests, ghost-thin, and at last,
in anesthetic dark, painlessly he tooths
the sweet flesh from the bones of his own hand.

All this I knew, without what you call horror,
but since he meant to horrify, I chose anger,
and thereafter, it is true, he was a wolf.
All one to me were his turns and swervings,
confession, lies, indifference, remorse.
Say that I showed him heavily how I saw him
from above: no wanderer but a map, unmoving.
Though a man thinks he can hide in changes.

Classic Bar Scenes

I. Apollo at Happy Hour

Shoulders and faint sheen
of lotion, torsion,

loose dress sliding
over flanks of glass,

silks so utterly watery
splashing, as you click along the shine,
on left shin right shin, but alas

the chase is a tired
and tiring metaphor:

let's sit. It is
your Beauty that is omnipotent,

and I the god its constant
victim, automatic

as the keyboard you reach over
accidentally typing with a breast
aaaaiiiiyyyyesssss,

as the copier you press
with a page and another page
that lights again and again your face.

Hear my song:
I will walk out of the 14th floor
and into your ear like a wireless call.

II. Ovidian Deposition

The bull or swan,
face rippling as it changes,
speaks, and for a long, long moment,
you can't tell luck from disaster.

He recited his exploits and cutting-edge features,
all the arts and countries he was lord of.

He was wasted, I think. He walked on the table.
He said his voltage was so out of control.

He said, *Relax, what you're feeling is*
the great experiences are generic:
when they happen to you they do not happen to you.

To take the god was to lose the man.
To take the man was to die of the god.
Either might turn me into stone.

I got up *For a refill*
from the Heliconian well,
and texted from the parking structure
Hadda go...

III. Pygmalion among the Young

He could tell from their pistol shots of laughter,
their bucking and surging
like someone learning to drive stick,
their pretense and collapse,
their talking on two cells at once,

how they down strange solvents,
their voices sax-raw or helium-high,
how they take each other harshly,
grinding together like stones,
grinding alone like stones, that the young
have statues in them, tall white statues
they must dance out, drink to sleep, outspeed.

Like a finger moving under a line of type—
O god, slower than that—
their future comes, the party they're late for
where people are saying incredible shit about them
that they have to get to, and say, and say
like how it really is, so they pile in and floor it
till their backs stiffen and their faces change in the wind.

IV. Twilight of a God

That girl who drank from her hands
huge wastes of wine,

and his awe,
was it? So that he surfaced,
his head in a little clear spot above the music

and a good bet was
that whatever happened next
wasn't going to happen to him.

Suddenly he wasn't the minor deity,
coat still on, in the corner booth,
smiling benevolently upon his children,

but a guy walking out, head down,
into the cold of an outer borough,
the signs unreadable, the age of Changes over.

Though aren't those still his angels
at the gold bar of Heaven
who lift glass trumpets to their lips?

V. Orpheus at Last Call

One of those dreams: you struggle and fail
for years
to dial a number, read a page, remember
not to look back...

(her hand confused in mine, soft struggle of a bird)

I've drunk so much
it rises in me: something like soft roots
parts softly
and my head sweeps down the singing river singing...

VI. Apollo in Age

Spring,

      I am no good with pain.
Stop,
      I'll tell you anything.

Zeus: A Press Conference

Eons we rule in our tall pale closets
and all your talk is the few failures of distance
even a man can read, in Ovid, in a few hours:
brute swan, tsunami of gold, bull
sliding the girl shark-swift into open sea.
The robe drops, the sun widens to half the sky,
the tachycardic certainty of death...

So similar the stories, maybe all one.
Whereas a god, on a million channels,
is all thoughts always. Once a millennium, maybe,
in his whited-out daydream he meets dark eyes
and is rapt into an endless morning after:
one man, one thought, one cup of coffee
for what, to a god, feels like a millennium.

You vultures, if you have to write, write
this: the humiliation of a human story
no god, with all Time, has the time to live,
or even read to the end. No questions.

State-Sponsored

Oh dear, say the Tyrants, *sex*
is naughty and intense
and might save you.
Please mistake it
for what you're not supposed to do.

Echo

And since she could only say back what she heard,
she had to listen for what she needed to say.
She haunted the edges of schoolyards first. Not it.
Lovers' lanes: hopeless. Cell phones seemed promising,
but really. She started reading novels
to put herself in the way of secret lives. It was the old story,
speed that was made to be followed, not repeated:
she remembered the ends of sentences, of sentences.

Why hasn't anyone said...? she thought, but couldn't say it.
What I want is... lilies in time-lapse bloomed, faces, explosions,
which she tried repeating. Stares, curious at least.
And if it had never in all history been uttered
would accident help her? She tried mishearing
flags snapping in darkness, the rumble of subways,
misquoting the birds even, two-wit, twang-a-wire, sorry-sorry.
Not quite, but there was something deep within them:

hadn't it been there at the world's beginning,
a silence? Yes, she could hear it still. It was like,
like a dumbstruck boy who looked at her as blankly
as if she were a pool, or he was, it was a question
spreading out larger and smoother, time itself,
to which she could hardly wait to hear her answer.

Bit Parts

In that monster epic of the checkout girl
I'm the guy setting groceries on the belt
in order of decreasing density, or maybe the one
whose *Did you get that coupon?* is the last straw,
so she streams out, shedding her smock, through automatic doors.

In that later movie of the two old friends
stopped dead in the whitewater of the crowd
with sudden love, I'm the *Excuse me* sidestepping them,
or the waiter they hardly see, clacking down two plates
with tolerant amusement, which is my specialty.

And in the film of the autumnal Liebestod,
I'm the guy sliding her the desperate ticket,
the arm hailing a taxi against the sunset,
the blink of a bike going by. If you notice me at all
you never ask *Who is that?* just

What else was he in? since I am small, and they
are large, these lovers, comets, and so swift,
fast-forwarding their whole lives in two hours,
hair blown back, that their whispers, stooping to us,
would be sonic booms, their hot touch catastrophic.

I sit, hand on your arm, as the Wave of the Century,
some poor lifeboat poised on its crest
like a sparrow lost in the whited-out sky,
collapses, a terrible powder of light
against the screen, roaring, leaving us dry.

I'm the abrupt laugh, or the back of a dark coat
up which, like rain on a windshield, climb the credits.
I am that faint curve graphed on the sand
in wrack and paper cups and foam that shows,
as the light comes up, how far the night had risen.

The God Who

It was the small gods we talked to
before words, though soon enough
we forgot, and sadly, that what dawn
or the shine of hips made the heart do
was prayer.
            The god of a particular
slow bend in the river, his friend
god of the white boats swung around it,
gods of moderately impressive rocks,
of spots warm where someone was just sitting,
of the deep sharp scents of shoes, of sounds
whose direction is unclear, of silver linings:
they appreciated whatever small appreciations
came their way and, ignored,
were not so much vengeful
as doubtful in that early world,
where the workload, if it can be called that,
of their divinely inefficient bureaucracy,
left plenty of time to enjoy the specialties
of their fellows, god of just sitting around,
god of the nasty slider, of low-battery gleeps,
of wine that gets better by the glass,
the god (the high god!) of too excited to sleep.

Actually, with considerable power
over one thing, or a couple—a book maybe,
tennis, unusual salads—but only average
at, say, getting lovers or starting a car,
they were a lot like us. Distinctions, in fact,
were not rigidly maintained, it being proverbially
difficult to be sure you're immortal
or that you're not. There was intermarriage,
bargaining, and respectful confusion (once
language got going)
about what constituted worship

and what was just delighted
saying of the names of things,
which persists. So as for the god

of the squeak of clean hair,
of your hand out the car window
wind-lifted, of the small shades under hat brims
and not excluding
the banned gods of leaf-fires and tobacco,

oh and definitely including
she of the coffee-breath and fine cold hands
who says *Sit down friend and let's see,
let's just see,* and certainly
my other god, he of Least Resistance
who decrees what is going to happen anyway,
who listens only to prayers that end
Let all be as Thou will'st, who grants
only my wish to believe in him,

and with the possible exception only of the god of making a list
of all the other gods, who gets distracted and forgets so many
that suddenly the universe is His and only His,

praise them.

II. Vectors 3.0

Vectors 3.0: Even More Aphorisms and Ten-Second Essays

1.

The odds against today were insurmountable, until it happened.

2.

If you can't take the first step, take the second.

3.

Experience afraid of its innocence is useless: no one is rich who cannot give his riches away.

4.

Spontaneity takes a few rehearsals.

5.

The days are in order, the months, the seasons, the years. But the weeks are work. They have no names; they repeat.

6.

Nothing dirtier than old soap.

7.

Office supplies stores are the cathedrals of Work in General. They forgive, they console, they promise a new start. These supplies have done work like yours a million times. Take them home and they will do it *for* you.

8.

When it gets ahead of itself, the wave breaks.

9.

Few plans survive their first success, which suggests they were less about their goals than about the possibility of a little success.

10.

The heart is a small, cracked cup, easy to fill, impossible to keep full.

11.

Hard disk: the letter I remembered as embarrassing is OK after all. I must have revised it just before sending. I never confuse what I dreamed with what I actually did, but this is different: which *draft* am I?

12.

Work is required play.

13.

My mistakes are not mine, but they are embarrassing because you might mistake them for my sins, which are.

14.

Perfection is besieged. Happier is the man who has done just a little better than he expected.

15.

How proud we are of our multitasking. What is Life but something to get off our desks, cross off our lists?

16.

I find my marginalia in an old book and realize that for decades I've been walking in a circle.

17.

The reader lives faster than life, the writer lives slower.

18.

Snakes cannot back up.

19.

First frost, first snow. But winter doesn't really start till you're sure that spring will never come.

20.

No one in human history has ever written exactly this sentence. Or anyway these two.

21.

Nothing important comes with instructions.

22.

The modesty of avoiding repetition is the vanity of thinking they must have been listening the first time.

23.

It can't hurt to ask is a phrase favored by those who can't quite tell people from institutions, thinking of both as randomly dispensing or refusing favors. Actually, it hurts me to be treated like a slot machine, maybe enough to pass the hurt along to you.

24.

I need someone above me—the Committee, the Law, Money, Time—to be able to say No. Sad my lack of integrity, though I suppose it would be sadder to need them to say Yes.

25.

The knife likes to think of itself as a mirror.

26.

The tyrant's self-esteem is just fine, thank you. It's you he doesn't care much for. And yes, he recognizes that he doesn't feel what you feel. Which is a good thing, since your feeling is so weak that it makes him need to beat you up.

27.

Self-sufficiency clings... to itself.

28.

He's angry at the wronged for making the world unjust.

29.

If you do more than your share you'd better want to: otherwise
you're paying yourself in a currency recognized nowhere else.

30.

The ascetic's last pleasure is blaming you for all he has forgone.

31.

There are two kinds of people in the world... and who is not
both of them?

32.

Beware speaking of The Rich as if they were someone else.

33.

We've learned to wonder which neutralizes truth more effec-
tively, the tyranny's censorship or the democracy's ten thousand
media outlets. In the former truth is too costly, in the latter
there's no market for it. In Freud the facts get around the cen-
sor in the metaphors of dreams, in Shelley we live in a dream of
overfamiliarity and dead metaphor that only the poet can reviv-
ify. Does repetition emphasize or hypnotize? Which is clearer,
what we see or what we don't see. Are we new or old? Do we
love hate or hate love?

34.

You have two kinds of secrets. The ones only you know. The
ones only you don't.

35.

Somehow the guy who's really interested in absolutely every-
thing is really boring.

36.

Sophistication is upscale conformity.

37.

The mirror's so quick it only sees what's in front of it.

38.

Knowing how to be pleased with what's there is a great secret
of happy living, sensitive reading, and bad writing.

39.

If you think you might be lost, you are. If you know you're
lost, you're at least free to look for the way.

40.

What keeps us deceived is the hope that we aren't.

41.

Everything is about politics. No, wait: everything is about sex.
Money, art, God, self, work.

42.

For those who tread lightly enough the air is a stair.

43.

I often find myself intoning Clarke's *Any sufficiently advanced
technology is indistinguishable from magic,* or anyway half of
it, since everyone's heard it already and interrupts. Actually the
technology doesn't have to be very advanced. I drive a car and
grasp the basics of internal combustion engines but I still treat
mine as halfway between pet and malevolent deity, muttering
reassurances, curses and spells. Maybe a chip designer gets
computers well enough that they are purely technology, but he

can't know that much about meteorology or gene-splicing or, well, poems. What differentiates technology from magic is not our knowledge but our faith: that someone else understands.

44.
Clarity is neither transparency nor light. It's the angle that suddenly lets you see through the window's glare, the pond's reflections.

45.
Faith is broad. It's Doubt that's deep.

46.
How badly I'd like to believe that my cherished moderation and heavily defended calm could rule the world. But as things are, somebody has to feel too much, somebody has to speak too loud, somebody has to be completely unreasonable.

47.
Don't trust the revolutionist with your freedom: he's an authoritarian who just happens to be out of power.

48.
Patience is easiest when it's the best way to make Impatience really mad.

49.
Is he talking about world hunger or just hungry to talk, is he angry at injustice or just angry, is he ruled by conscience or does he just need to rule mine? Probably my scruple about purity of Faith is irrelevant, but so, if the standard is Good Works, are his words.

50.
Listen hardest to the one you hope is not telling the truth.

51.

The coy and impotent self-importance of *subversive*. A bunch of kids in black who can't think of anything better to talk about between drags than how uncool their parents are.

52.

Thoughts are discussed, opinions displayed.

53.

The peril of arguing with you is forgetting to argue with myself. Don't make me convince you: I don't want to believe that much.

54.

Tyranny and fantasy both like to write everyone else's lines.

55.

He prides himself on having lots of opinions, like bad moods he's entitled to. Worse than stupidity is intelligence that claims the right to be stupid.

56.

No one blames you for having your dream, just for telling it.

57.

Everyone's psyched that elections are decided by a single vote! That it's a close game! That choice approximates chance!

58.

The lesser of two evils is the one with the less evil friends.

59.

How comforting, your paranoia: someone's listening, some-one's watching, someone's thinking about you all the time.

60.

Build bottom up, clean top down.

61.

Precision strike. We're only killing that one guy. And actually only his worst thought. And there, just a little to the left of the middle, only the very worst part of that.

62.

The fire doesn't know where all that smoke came from.

63.

The patterned shirt, the speckled wall-to-wall *don't show dirt*. Sometimes, truth be damned, we need relief from seeing. Our response is a bigger problem than the problem.

64.

Forgive the evil done to you. Really? I can't help thinking the Book just didn't trust me enough to say what it meant: *In time you will see that much of it was not evil, and that much of the evil was yours.*

65.

Too much apology doubles the offense.

66.

Forgiveness is freedom, the saints say, but they are saints and do not care that it may be freedom even from love.

67.

All those days that changed the world forever! Yet here it is.

68.

Let us explain to ourselves the difference. A rock might be very big, like Plymouth Rock or the Rock of Gibraltar. Or under-ground, as in bedrock. A rock is rough. A stone is smooth: it might well be cut into a gravestone, a cobblestone. Rocks you clamber over, stones you step on. What's that brilliance on her finger, a rock or a stone? The rock-thrower is anonymous. Let him who is without sin cast the first stone.

69.

Do unto others and an eye for an eye have the same payment plan.

70.

For Sisyphus the trouble of pushing the rock uphill was worth it for the thrill of watching it smash everything on the way down.

71.

That little bird, pretty calm there in the snow, is cold, but it must be a discontinuous and lightly registered sensation. *Cold. Peck peck. What's that? Oh yeah, cold.* Whereas I would be desperate in a few minutes thinking about freezing Forever and Ever. Somewhere in evolution we traded endurance for foresight. Intelligence was first of all the ability to worry.

72.

That half-second between stubbing your toe and convulsing with pain? Some live there forever.

73.

We ask *What's the worst that could happen?* see that it wouldn't be so bad, calm down a little. What I want to know is: what is that *Worse than the Worst* we have to figure out over and over is *not* going to happen?

74.

The squirrel struggling in the road. Something very deep says *If it can't live it should die.* I kill it with a stick. Maybe to stop my own suffering, but I don't think so: I'd rather walk away. Maybe Nature wants me to think this way about my own kind? The thought struggles in me. I kill it with a stick.

75.

Stones, toys, ants, birds, children: the more we decide is less than human, the less human we become.

76.

Her grief repeats with a high cracked sound, like an engine in which something has broken loose and is smashing around. People scare us when they're like machines, when they're so *human*.

77.

If we were really sure of our freedom we wouldn't be so discomfited by those who make passion a habit, or habit a passion.

78.

Slug, fungus: part of your body has fallen out. Snake, rat: part of it might try to get back in.

79.

Treasury reports that its green ink absorbs opiates: every bill carries ten nanograms of cocaine. Amazing what this might be made to say about several addictions, but I'm going to stop right now.

80.

Roadkill. Something eats the eyes first, starved for... what?

81.

The rich man thought he was hoarding freedom, but he couldn't stop and in the end it all turned out to be money.

82.

Last Day say all the stores.

83.

In a strange city, my one tenuous root is a lit room in Hotel X. Passing Hotel Y, I imagine taking a room there as well, traveling away from my travel, pure waste, lost or free, whatever the difference is. Has anyone ever done this and managed to get home? Please write.

84.

Of course I'm an escapist. I'm trying to get somewhere real.

85.

It's not that they give things of no worth: that, too, is giving. It's what they want for them.

86.

The Victorian hotel has a marble colonnade, gilt, oriental rugs, but there's not a tux in sight: shirts-out-over-jeans mix with business suits. Is it freedom that we no longer have to dress up to such elegance, or is it history-is-ours arrogance? Probably it's more that life now is a theme park: when you visit Disney World you don't dress as Mickey or Goofy.

87.

Tragedy and comedy ended with death or marriage, but our shows, mystery and sitcom, begin with them.

88.

We don't blame the victim, already murdered when the show starts. We don't even blame the perp too much—we just want to find out who he is. We don't blame the cops for blaming him. Best of all, we don't blame ourselves, so trivial our own crimes in comparison. And if anyone wants to blame us we've got a perfect alibi for prime time.

89.

You have the right to lie when they have no right to ask.

90.

Since God died, no one has remembered you. But now it seems your DNA is everywhere and could be followed like a trail, if you could just act suspicious enough.

91.

He spends minutes looking for a parking place that shortens his walk by seconds, days looking for a price lower by an hour's wage, as if he would otherwise be *fooled*.

92.

The boutique wants you to think you're collecting, the discounter that you're stealing.

93.

The thing about the natural world, beautiful or bleak or bleakly beautiful, is that nothing seems to be in the wrong place. From this window, however, I can see the trowel I left in the yard, and I'm going to have to go down and do something about it.

94.

The way your walk changes entering a store or museum, slowing, widening a little, eyes sweeping level. Foraging on the ancient savanna for something to eat, something to use.

95.

The Mystery we're absorbed in takes precedence over all the mysteries that won't be solved when the hour ends, a protective parenthesis within the larger stories of Love and Work, which are inside the story of Life, which is inside Big Bang. Actually scale is irrelevant: it's just as likely we'd use cosmology to distract us from a bad day at the office. Theoretically all these are contained within a larger Storylessness, but that itself is only the romantic story *I have at last attained freedom,* which in an instant decays into more stable stories such as *I'm so bored I'd rather be afraid* or *I must punish the deluded masses with this hard truth* or *Let's watch TV.*

96.

From the tipped tree you learn how shallow roots are. More meets the eye than doesn't.

97.

Joe Cool is playing at Cold. And his babe is Hot, which is also play, and in that more like Cool than like Warm: no one exclaims delightedly "Man, that's *Warm!*" We'll pay to watch the players of Hot and Cool, but we flee the salesmen, priests and politicians solemnly emitting Warm.

98.

That our feelings flicker so obviously in our faces must mean Nature thought it was more important that everyone be able to read them than that individuals be able to hide them. Maybe it tells us, too, that the most dangerous faces are the ones behind which there is no feeling at all.

99.

Glasses, for example, have gone from uptight to wide-eyed and back again. Fashion is feeling, opening and closing, cycling between warm and cool, welcoming and slick. Or rather, it decides which half of feeling will be paraded, which half will seem hidden, and somehow truer.

100.

The sun's so bright it has no face.

101.

Yet sometimes maybe I decide to let an emotion I really could conceal flit faintly across my face. If it seems I betrayed it unwillingly, you are less likely to respond as if you had seen it.

Though maybe that little bit of acting is not really a conscious strategy but a deep instinct: in the animal world, too, emotions are often merely theatrical, and so many threats, fake fights and sexual displays send messages but end in nothing.

102.

More and more graduates of the School of Theatrical Parenting. The guy being a Good Father so loudly we can all appreciate him, the woman with the wailing infant rolling her eyes as if to say "Can you *believe* this baby?"

103.

Passion is faintly rhetorical, as if we needed to convince ourselves we were capable of it.

104.

Am I trying to help, or do I just want you to like me? The way feelings are, it's not so easy to distinguish your happiness from mine.

105.

Her grief is eased when all grieve with her, his when he sees that grief is only his.

106.

I say *Be reasonable* when I am afraid to feel what you feel.

107.

A feather lands on the pond and a dozen goldfish come to poke at it. We are whoever rises into our eyes to have a look.

108.

Those so thorough you cannot in mercy ask them to do anything. Those so empathetic it is cruel to tell them a trouble.

109.

As a couple they are salt of the earth, sodium chloride. As single elements, she was a poisonous gas and he a soft and desperate metal, turning even water into roil and flame.

110.

When we talk it's not you or me we are getting to know. It may be nothing at all, it may be better than both of us.

111.

Don't touch, don't stare. But no one minds how hard you listen.

112.

No one so entertaining as the one who thinks you are.

113.

The Boy wants magical powers. He wants the world to respond gigantically to every little thing he does and says, and even all he doesn't say and do. Until he meets the Girl who does just that.

114.

Loving yourself is about as likely as tickling yourself.

115.

That book, that woman, life: now that I understand them a little I realize there was something I understood better when they baffled and scared me.

116.

A knot is strings getting in each other's way. What keeps us together is what keeps us apart.

117.

Nostalgia for a Lost Love. At a certain distance the parts of you and her that could never love each other become invisible, which is how you got into that whole mess in the first place.

118.

My loss is sad: I have not yet lost it all.

119.

Finally peace. And then the whisper: *Does that passion work anymore?* I'll wake it up and see...

120.

The will has a will of its own.

121.

It is with poetry as with love: forcing yourself is useless, you have to want to. Yet how tiresome and ungenerous is the one sprawled among flowers waiting for his impulse. There's such a thing as knowing how to make yourself want to.

122.

Our resolutions for self-control are like our wars for peace.

123.

Freedom has just escaped. Peace has forgotten. Boredom is pounding on the prison gates to be let back in.

124.

To begin the journey, buy what you need. To finish, discard what you don't.

125.

As for my writing. I like it enough to keep going. I dislike it enough to keep going.

126.

What hope we had when we knew everything would last for-
ever, and what hopelessness.

127.

Now the mail is not *Hope* but *What Do They Want from Me?*
I still fetch it, perhaps knowing that someday I'll be reduced to
hoping they still want something from me.

128.

It takes thick gloves, prying down to the knotty junction,
getting as many of the roots as I can, to take care of them for
maybe a year, the brambles. But I'm avoiding the point, pas-
torally, which is the dull-witted malignancy that's taking you
over, that there's no scalpel precise enough to excise one bad
cell at a time, no chemotherapy bomb smart enough to kill
them all without killing you. I need to be a gardener small
enough to pull out one by one the runners that are re-wiring
you. Here, the gods have granted my wish but I am just as
helpless, hands bloodier and bloodier as I work far into the
night. There are acres and acres to go before that little rise
where the thorns have overgrown the castle where you are
struggling not to sleep. I can do this, I can do whatever is
necessary. It won't take forever, nothing takes forever, but so
many things take longer than we have.

129.

Of course when I look in the mirror I see what was there 10,
20, 30 years ago. It's not just vanity, dear: I see through you the
same way.

130.

The myths tell us what we already know: that it will be the last
light left burning, waking us even after death. Seems I have
spent my whole life fleeing Judgment, and yet I must not believe
in it, since no failure, no betrayal forces me to admit *Yes, at last
that is myself.* What a strange relief it would be to finally hit

that bottom, a hypochondriac who learns at last what he will
die of.

131.
Behind your face, which hardly changes, who knows what
thoughts. It's the opposite with the gods: their powers and
stories are constant, but painters give them random faces.

132.
That letter, what would it have been, of love, of praise, of anni-
hilating understanding? It seems, almost sadly, that I no longer
want to get it. Occasionally I still want to write it, but how
could I send to anyone else what I would not myself receive?

133.
Alas, how quickly my sincerest praise turns into apology for
secret doubts.

134.
Faces are motion, which is why all the photos of you are bad.
Even the most natural-looking portrait is a sentence inter-
rupted. And faces in motion hide an even deeper motion. You
seem to sit there and meet my eyes across the table, but you
are so many other places, clinging here for a moment against
all the currents that will soon sweep you onward. We are so
moved by the faces caught in the windows of trains going the
other way because they tell us how all faces really are.

135.
A very few people have seen me only at my best. They are
precious friends, but I dare not meet them again.

136.
What was it like before language? My occasional thought,
more than urge but still less than words, that would translate as
Eat now, there may be no food where we're going.

137.

Out walking, I think of that face I love or some scene of awful
embarrassment and stop dead in my tracks, as if I had to
choose between moving and being moved.

138.

Clarity, even in person, can be pretty hard. Telephones are
harder: if I can't see your eyes, how do I know what I'm saying?
With writing, misunderstandings multiply, since tiny shifts in
tone and speed are no longer audible—the writer tries to com-
pensate by managing rhythm and punctuation and deploying a
larger and more nuanced vocabulary than we need for speech.
Along comes e-mail and from all sides the complaint that it is a
peculiarly toneless genre that regularly offends and annoys and
misinforms. Though screens are not as stable as pages, e-mail
is not essentially different from other writing. The difference is
us: we write it too quickly, we read it even more quickly. A lot
of e-mails are work, to be gotten out of the way. And even the
young, who grew up with it—especially the young, who grew
up with it—seem incapable of reading further than three sen-
tences before flapping off into some heaven of *I already know
this.* Not a problem if the e-mailers or texters are in constant
chat and so deep in a shared context that misunderstanding can
be averted with crude steering like smiley face and LOL, or if
they're using the form as a kind of contentless *I was here,* the
way people used to leave their cards. But the temptation is to
e-mail little essays. The temptation is, worse, to try to replace
our unpredictable and wounding social drama with writing:
the protection of its distance, the smoothness of its infinite
rehearsals. But who has the patience to be a good writer all
day? Inevitably, we *send* too soon and get back reports of the
damage. I resolve to quit e-mail and get a life. Or maybe just
do one more revision. Thanks for reading to the end.

139.

Of course we want to write what we loved reading over and
over. That's different from constructing an Object of Study,
which is sort of like baiting a trap with staples or capacitors.

Such contraptions subsist on the praise of those who want permission for similar self-indulgences, even though the only mice ever seen near them are mechanical.

140.

When you think in words, are you sure it's your own voice you hear?

141.

I want to kill the guy dominating the train with his cell phone. What's his problem, pathetic self-importance or pathetic dependence? Ah well, maybe if we still had real lives we'd all be gabbing around the fire, gossiping at the pump. What's remarkable, after all, is not his self-important prattle but that someone is listening to it. Or so I've assumed: maybe there's really no one on the other end?

142.

Solitude: that home water whose sweetness you taste only when you've been someone else too long.

143.

The audience is faceless, back rows disappearing into dimness, and it doesn't talk back. *Find your audience* and you will blather. Write, instead, to the listener at your table for two, the one in your head whose faint blush, half-smile, glazed eyes make you correct course in midsentence, back off, explain, stop to listen.

144.

Fame is underwritten by those who want it to be there when it is their turn to have it.

145.

Old radios hummed a little before they could think what to say, their deep interiors like embers blown on. They told the great stories, in them the great stars sang. New radios, sleek and compulsively chatty, instantly repeat what they have heard. The TV, their doe-eyed younger sister, grew up adored. She wants so much to be looked at that you stare at your feet, abashed. She says *Have a drink with me,* and then *I'm so lonely that I can love nothing. Stay for another.*

146.
It is the empty seats that listen most raptly.

147.
The great man's not sure he wants you to criticize even his great rival, lest there be no such thing as greatness.

148.
Talking to yourself is not the same as talking to no one.

149.
I'm forced to admit I'm second-rate: I don't have the genius's certainty about who he is. And when I talk myself into that certainty? I'm third-rate.

150.
It's not success but self-congratulation that the Furies scent.

151.
Would it have been better or worse if I could have whispered to myself back then *I know the way. Follow me. But it will take 30 years.*

152.
My best critic is me, too late.

153.
I look over my old books, happiest when I find a line it seems I could not have written.

154.

Only your unnoticed victories last: the rest are avenged.

155.

I'm scared of the huge ocean—what prevents it from throwing itself over me and the tiny continents? So much harder to see what's holding *others* back.

156.

By spending so much on insurance—medical, car, fire, disability, retirement, termite, appliance—I try to make every year average. I guarantee that I'll be perennially slightly short of cash in the hope that I'll never be totally broke. A mortgage, broadly speaking, is also a kind of insurance—against ever having to ask *Where shall I lie down?* Other kinds of payments ensure more or less constant answers to the questions of who to be, who to be with, what to do, whether to live.

157.

What is more yours than what always holds you back?

158.

What I can't do at all is no trouble. But save me from what I do pretty well with disproportionate effort and distortion of soul. For that I am in Hell.

159.

Is this poetry? Is the tomato a fruit? Yes to a botanist, no to someone making a fruit salad. If the world is divided into poetry and prose, this is prose. If it's divided into fiction, nonfiction, and poetry, this is poetry.

160.

The gods give no credit for the good deeds I complain about doing.

161.

All my life I've been working on an excuse no one will ever want to hear.

162.

The sinner hopes there is no God. The just man looking at the world thinks there cannot be. The lazy man just can't imagine anyone wanting the job.

163.

I've lived here so long I trip on what has been gone for years.

164.

How do you know life is not a dream? Because things change so slowly. Because you can focus on a page or dial a number, and when you go back to your study for your glasses, there they are, just where you left them. Because you can't fly and they don't come back from the dead. Because so often you want to believe that life is a dream.

165.

I shorten my life by imagining it's too late for everything I really didn't want to do anyway.

166.

No one has yet failed in the future.

167.

At first skepticism keeps you from being too much like everyone else, then, you hope, from being too much like yourself.

168.

Sure, no one's listening, English will die in a hundred years, and the far future is stones and rays. But here's the thing, you Others, you Years to Come: you do not exist.

169.

That one thing in Life I'm meant to do?—well, I have to finish this first.

170.

Closing a door very gently, you pull with one hand, push with the other.

III. By the Numbers

By the Numbers

One, says the bell,
and one and one.
The window no one sees through
is the sun.

One and then two
will count up shoes,
two then one
counts seconds down.

Three is a crowd,
three four your slim
fingers on a glass
(plus thumb).

Crows argue:
Five, eight, FIVE.
(Owl doubts:
two one, two who?)

Clock separates
with six six six,
the click
of icy sticks on sticks.

Seven's the heaven
that eight is late for,
and nine's a tulip
tense in wind.

Or ten is hands
lined with journeys,
and nine means one
has fallen behind.

Eight times this page
in half and in half
my strength can fold
(or only seven).

And six, then five,
the deer like smoke
fade through pines
dark rises in.

And quarry's four,
or hunted *coeur,*
and three is odd,
they say, the crowd

that heart counts up
or heart counts down,
old juggler dropping
one one one…

And countless you!
The moon, a door
you stand half in,
lights one dark shoe.

Birds in Rain

Studious silence in the trees.
Later they will tunefully dispute
whether the drops came down in twos or threes.

Are We Alone?
or
Physics You Can Do at Home

The simplest and most popular cosmological model today predicts that you have a twin in a galaxy about 10 to the 10^{28} meters from here... In infinite space, even the most unlikely events must take place somewhere.

*

Searches for extraterrestrial intelligence have at least partially scanned for Earth-level radio transmitters out to 4,000 light-years... and for... advanced civilizations out to 40,000 light-years... The lack of signals is starting to worry many scientists.

That momentary tightening of your voice
over your cheerfully expiring cup of steam, maybe it's nothing—
always the vanishingly small but nonzero probability

all protons in the room might decay spontaneously,
a little run in the sheer black of the universe
unzip to the utter nothing of the Beginning.

Ninety minutes is the length of a mood, according to scientists,
and the lifespan of a universe. One wrong turn and the metropolis
in the rear view goes dark, the love that turns wrong never was.

In the advanced geometry of gravity wells and higher dimensions
two points apparently close may be separated by eons,
parallel realities by less than the thickness of a page,

though an unturnable page. Two sitting together may be infinitely distant,
while two on different continents staring into books may startle
as the lines of their gazes cross glancingly deep in the planet.

If space is infinite, as it may well be, and if you and I
are protons arranged in a pattern of, once again, vanishingly low
but not zero probability, as we certainly are,

mere odds say we have twins in a galaxy 10 to the 10^{28} meters from here,
which is a very long walk, though even so you may feel their gray light
in the back of your mind, the blur in your shoulders of being shadowed,

since certain processes, such as the expansion of space itself, quantum entanglement,
(which Einstein called *spooky action at a distance*), hope, portent and
        embarrassment,
unlimited by the speed of light, can be virtually instantaneous.

The odds say somewhere C, the heroine I loved, is on my side of the page,
and somewhere I never read her book, and somewhere I wrote it,
since everything has happened somewhere, everything has happened once,

though more locally astronomers have scanned for simple radio transmissions
out to 4,000 light-years, and for supercivilizations to 40,000, and the silence
is starting to worry them (but I am worried more about that intergalactic sense

that someone has already lived my life—but how?—or I am living it for someone—
        who?),
and even more locally Heisenberg says I cannot know both your position and
        momentum
though you cell me saying where, and from your breathlessness I guess how fast.

On the largest scale ordinary matter is outnumbered five to one by Dark Matter,
not a single particle of which has yet been detected, though a million
stream through an area the size of a quarter, your eye, your lips, each second—

yes, another form of touch we failed to guess at, chargeless,
interacting with us only through gravity, which is what holds us together,
but is sadly by orders of magnitude the weakest force in the universe:

for example, I lift my cup, countering the entire gravitational field
of the earth's six sextillion tons with a calorie of electrochemical energy
I maybe flossed from my teeth and swallowed all unawares.

Yes, since 1998 it has been known that gravity is failing us
and the expansion of the universe, governed by a principle of distraction called Dark
    Energy,
which constitutes 72% of everything, though like Dark Matter it is so far undetected,

is accelerating, proving... what escapes me... and this sense of things going downhill
faster than expected is the cause for what we previously thought was our baseless
    worry
and the true answer to the formerly soothing question *What's the worst that could
    happen?*

But let's get practical. At sublight speed I may not catch my train this morning,
the fauna are comfortably repetitive, the same cars pass, numbered the same,
and I can't see the galaxies fleeing. For all I know, some nights they steal closer, just as

though I take the entropy of the body for granted, it can't be measured in the
    short run,
and maybe sometimes in half-darkness, when the machines aren't looking,
we grow younger for a while. But large trends, the odds say, cannot be resisted
    indefinitely.

Yes, the odds talk unstoppably... they say intelligent species have arisen
very near us and are gone, and will arise again very near, maybe here, when we are
    gone,
and the practical problem is only that space travel is slow and civilizations merely a
    blink

in the life of the universe, so even though they have looked for us, and even now
are on their way, and though we have looked for them, well, the central issue in
    cosmology
and several less arcane disciplines is that there simply isn't enough time,

and if we ever find them, which odds say we won't,
they will, odds are, be dead and gone. And if they find us, any of them—
and odds are many will—we will be gone, surely long dead and gone.

And the odds say... sorry... the odds keep saying disconnected possibilities,
so fast they are simultaneous, for example that a quintillion atoms
in your body are replaced every second, changing practically nothing,

and that the universe may be the 3-D sheen on a wineglass of $4 + n$ dimensions,
and all the information on the Internet, considered as electrons, weighs a millionth of
    an ounce,
less than a fingerprint, a tear, and in the modern world time is the accumulation of
    information,

which is officially the same as the loss of information, which is time,
and somehow always at the end a hand raised *Oh sorry a question we do not have
    time for,*
because we are late for something else we apparently have time for.

If classical physics held, electrons would wind down and crash into the nucleus in
    nothing flat,
trees holding out their arms would drop them to their sides in weariness,
and matter from sheer boredom would dissipate, but somehow we persist,

which is why I stayed home to watch the snow wash all connections out of the air,
and now, behind each stone and tree and behind my eyes, caverns narrowing into
    ellipses
deepen a little. All is further. Not sure I could move the hand at the end of my arm...

The closer you approach a black hole, the greater the weight of inevitability,
hardly time for a single decision, a single digit in the phone number you dreamily
and repetitively tried to dial all night—for help was it?—

though to an observer your vastly redshifted descent seems to take forever,
whereas standing right here your motion towards earth's center is continuously
    impeded,
since everything by nature—the atom, the mind—is trying to fall down a hole too
    small for it.

More practically, the vacuum is a foam of particles and antiparticles arising and can-
    celing each other,
just as my silence is words and antiwords canceling each other unspoken.
You could hear this faintly in the small hours, except for the turnpike whine,

because it's a big empty universe, averaging only five atoms per cubic meter,
though wherever we are is by definition very crowded. I think of walking out in the
    snow
which would then be very, very crowded, for though the air seems clear, glassy with
    silence,

odds say in every breath there's at least one atom of the breath of everyone who ever
    lived
and if to breathe them is to hold them all in mind,
which I hope is true... but surely this feeling of a thought being too big to think

is the accelerating expansion of the universe, which means I should try less and less
to think it, and be still like a tree letting stars and snow stream through its branches,
for scientists agree that not to think is to think everything, which is what the uni-
    verse excels at,

though with its expansion proceeding at a rate unguessable when we were young,
and the Law of Conservation of Mattering decreeing that the absolute quantity of
    mattering is fixed,
it follows that things on the average matter less and less.

Moreover Relativity says the faster you think, trying to keep up, the slower your
    time moves
in relation to a stationary observer, so if you are habitually close to the speed of
    light, like this,
those you loved will be agèd or dead when you finish with what you thought you
    had to do,

so here I am again after what seemed a minute's silence but could have been millions
    of your years.
Who knows if you or anyone I remember is the same, if I am the same
(sorry a question we do not have time for), and what we thought of as our moment

may have already passed into a cosmic morning-after, like that party my parents
    gave—
what, fifty years ago?—nebulae of wrapping, off-color joke gifts redshifted far be-
    yond me,
full ashtrays, drinks weak with icemelt, the shrill flat smell of faded excitement,

since everything has happened somewhere and everyone has happened once
(oh, let's not be sentimental, it has all happened over and over,
and if we find them they'll be gone, and when they find us we'll be gone),

and yes, at the moment, the world in which I began this sentence
is impossibly distant, and the world in which I have finished
and am condemned to what I have said, which is why it is called a sentence,

is impossibly distant but approaching, if that is not a metaphor, faster than light,
and here it is right now. Think of the mind as a device where universes—this one,
the one to the left, or a little later, or not quite—converge, which saves a lot of
    space,

zillions in superposition, fading in halos of regret, or collapsing un-imagined,
in a kind of reverse Big Bang, to just what Is, which saves really a lot of space.
Yes, even now I feel the expansion of space counteracted by dark unmattering,

and now, yes, the snow-blue is the blueshift of things moving closer and closer
    together,
and since anyway the most common compulsion, really the only one, is to begin
    again,
I need to ask, though it has been asked in a zillion ages and places, I will need
    to ask

in the universe rushing towards us (metaphorically) faster than the speed of light,
    the one
where we are together again: Well, is that coffee you've got there, steaming, or the
    hell of fusion
in the star-tight grip, in the tokamak of your cupped hands?

Prokaryotes

Say we found it on Europa,
DNA, an alien line,
could we wait a billion years to ask
How was it for you—
blue, that whiff of ammonia, Time?

The Stars in Order Of

The stars in order of
magnitude, of age,
of Pisces/Taurus/Gemini,
of stature, tilt, and price—
                              I mean
hot Sirius and gaudy Mars,
historic stars, and not
those pinpoint whites
we hurry under, no, not those

pixels. I mean stars
like dimes some kid threw
in the mall fountain,
or large
and soft as dandelions
or right here that
scatter of heat
on your face—yes, feeling,
what harm, spreading out?

                    *

Such stars it was
that *soldiers and poor*
of old and on stone pillows
lay beneath, naming
Scorpions and Hot Bods,
and I also once in
not quite love,
lying in a field and losing
and losing (and with what
pleasure-pain)
something into the sky—
                              I mean,
so young, I felt

in how many photons
per hour on the retina
amounts to Visible
an almost touch,
an almost face, their grass scent,
the sweep of a hem, or even,
I could think, the tiny strokes
of Fate they so long managed:

changing our hearts
with a little charge of light,
an arrow blinked awry
by a ray, a crucial messenger,
oh, like me,
lying down to dream
a little too long in the meadow
or, as here, please,
just long enough...

*

To stars on high
cloud-breathing
birds are crawling things,
their faces almost in the grass.
Almost we earthlings should,
stars think, smell the warm
leading-edge
of wings, smell
Moon, too,
where it has brushed
almost the grass, bending
to see itself in one
blade's tip's

dew.
Once even stars
were (again might be?)

once, yes, within the range
of vespers, *church-bells*
beyond the stars heard,

but they are shy
now of skyglow, clatter,
also our distraction
dims and deafens
them, us,

though maybe that
in-small-hours-faint roar
I think is turnpike, heartwash,
imagination
is them,

maybe in the lilac-ozone-rust
of complex air, their scent's
a faint strange animal,
its freeze with fear, or some
ellipsis of its trail...

*

That little clique
of six, or was it seven
Pleiades before
my haste, gray air and
softening eyes
took one? That some lands call

Chums of Artemis, some
Tortoise or Hen-and-Chicks,
some Summer-
Moves-to-Winter, and that now

sidelong I look for since
(stargazers know)

peripheral vision picks up
fainter things, though not
(for that: head-on)
not color.

But now, so tenuous
and unfelt of men are star-roots,
scythed by every
wings-flat glide
and umpire's arms-wide *Safe,*
they flee from us, and even

stars that linger,
with obvious color and what seemed
an interest in our fate,
yellow Saturn, angry Mars,
we know are cold, unbreathable,

even Venus, which
we'd still like to be Love—
well, it's 900 degrees
there and you can't get a drink
and that watery green the comics
thought was jungle,
if you keep looking,
is desert desert white.

*

Late as we are, most things
we know are burnt
like that, part spent. Most
of our elements—carbon,
oxygen—were fused from hydrogen
and helium in screwed-tight
wingnut starhearts,

and heavier traces

in our cells of copper, iodine,
selenium (not
what the word says, "moonmetal")
are atoms slammed tight
together in a star's collapse
and self-rebounding supernova,

yet nothing we remember
of their height, sublimity,
no aftertremor of their
sans peur raining down.

       *

Harder and more far
they seem
now we more need them...

Maybe in compensation,
astronomers lately
and sillily have named
southern constellations for
friendly mechanisms: Telescope,
Microscope and Cell Phone,
and on Valentine's
for 40 bucks you can call one
Seth or Jennifer, and apparently
no one will tell you not to—

what the heck,
100 billion in the galaxy,
about as many, so they say,
as neurons in the brain, also
as I predict (stars
on the brain) as many humans
as will ever
ever live and die: so each

name one, and let it go...

But Star (if it
were ours)
would share a root with
Steer. Doesn't.
Stare. Nope.
Stir. Not.
Sterile. Nunh unh.
Or else
only in the long
before-words when nothing
was but stars in order of
no order... otherwise,

Star comes
from an older word
meaning Star
which comes from an older word
meaning Star,
which comes from an older word
meaning Star.

Stars after all
(not flat the sky)
scatter at depths, and only
accidents of perspective

make strangers (as
also here on Earth)
seem to constellate.

They do not know

what story they are part of (same
with us), maiden
or monster (same)

floating in the
absolute cold
(we know),
in joy too cold

(their joy seems cold)
pure joy too cold for us.

*

Oddly no Constellations
are called Vast or Black
or Nearly Empty, none
Scattershot or Bunch of Dots,
nor were our ancestors
into abstraction, none called
Efficiency or Good Tidings
or Up Late Can't Stop,

not Slow Curve or
Eat Here, no writing
of any kind
(though we look for it), not

What Is Left, or
Day Too Quick to Open,
not Glance Unmet,
not What I Missed,

also there oddly
or not oddly is
no constellation Star...

Origin of Language

The Lord hummed quietly and hated Adam
singing out stupid names for the animals.

Songs for Senility

Names go first
(and *you* are?)
Sadly I confuse
bordering words:
awful, awesome,
property, happenstance,
lowered, lord.
What's the deference?

Silly is soul,
all Nancys blur,
all the King Henrys.
Who was it, Wordsworth
or Groucho, that said it:
All Men become Whosit.
All Things become Thingies.

All jets are black,
all crime violet.
Lemons are yellow
running over cliffs.
There's ice in service,
from is form,
and trite is tried is tired.

Once I could declare
that have and heave,
that lift and left
and gift... I had a point
here that I forget.
(I had a pint
and I forgot.)
Once I was sure
what was decay
and what was metaphor.
And *you* are?

*

I have lost
(oh what's the word?)
my keys?
To the Kingdom?
All Mythologies? The car?—
its color, greeny-gray
or purple-brown?
its parking space?
the city of whatsit it was in?
Which is just like love,
like a draining tub
or loosening belt
or brie en croûte
(this list was?—I forget).

*

Now that I'm not so smart...
others are smarter!
Now that I'm not so... whatever,
others are... yeah...

Now that I'm not so... uh...
I see everywhere—
in airports or stuffed chairs—
my exact double,

shortish, brown-gray, quiet,
my exact double,
though younger (everyone's younger),
my exact double.

My exact double except
his cap is a Mets cap,
except it's reversed,
except

he's Guatemalan,
he's a woman,
a cell-phone addict,
no, a psychotic

talking to himself,
my exact double
saying to air
his beautiful fears.

I wonder does he see
(my exact double)
that he's undoubtedly
my exact double.
I look into his eyes
that are looking different ways,
that are asking, as I ask,
And *you* are?

              *

Now that I'm not so good
at things I was great at,
great to do not so badly
things I'm not bad at.

That finely cut sandwich,
exceptional *hiya,*
much improved
taking letters out of the box
or shading my eyes, pretty good
getting into the car
with knees, perfectly timed
cutoff of a sales call
or catching of your drift

that ends up on all
the highlight shows,

he goes back he goes back
and against the wall...

...leaps.
          I'm too old to leap
Fosbury-style,
do a respectable backbend,
pitch for the Yankees,
run a four-minute mile
(always have been),

but maybe, who knows,
I can eat as fast as ever,
or play cards—
or maybe just try
unprecedented things
to hide my decline.
Hell, set some records:

most consecutive letters typed incorrectly,
most graceful stair-stumble recovery,
best gaze at this
not particularly interesting rock
while singing,
most efficient clearing
of cobwebs in this particular corner
on a Tuesday evening using one hand only
and singing, best imagining
I am singing beautifully
while not so beautifully singing.

                    *

Now that my memory's weak,
I spread things out on the desk.
Anything under
anything else: forget it.

Now that my memory's empty
I disbelieve in depth.
I close my eyes
to look deep in myself:
and *you* are?

Now that my memory leaks
and my real memory
is my hard disk:
what a relief!

Bad poems, delete.
Bad friends, bad letters,
bad days, blunders,
dumb things said drunk,
delete delete.

My most embarrassing
delete my half-assed
delete my pompous
delete delete
arrogance delete.

Yeats said he'd live it all again
but I delete
the ignominy of
delete *the distress* delete
the finished man among
delete delete.

Sorry, first wife I forget:
thanks for whatever.
Kind supporters,
great poets
I leaned on, awful poets:
I forget, sorry.

Neighbor who thoughtfully called
delete,

employer helpless
to fire me,
students I galled
delete delete.

Sorry parents, sorry early lovers,
I declare, sorry,
I am pastless and uncaused!
Nothing was my fault, sorry!

                    *

Delete delete
till I'm just my own
Greatest Hits.
But as for that,
why save the Heavens
I declined from?

Nine times the space that measures day and night
delete I land with a thud
wherever:
but O *how fall'n! how chang'd*
from... Huh?

                    *

It's best to travel light
(I don't remember why),
and less is more
(again, not sure).

Why hundreds of restrooms,
a billion spams, a thousand
heartbreaking faces
or cereal labels

when one delete delete
will do, or just a couple?

Since time is short
delete delete
and backpacks small,
let's simplify a little:

when such as I cast out
delete delete
it's all fine,
all fucking the same!
I've missed delete!
And lost delete!
Left nothing undone!

                    *

The woods decay,
the woods decay and fall,
and so do I, so yeah,
I worry about stumbling
through a dimensional flaw
into an alternate universe,
one all purple rays
or a giant airport terminal,
one that is light-years
of the interior of a pear—
worth seeing for a minute,
if I could get back.

But that's the trick.
There was a universe
where my shoulder brushed the jamb
of a small child's room
but I can't get back.

I remember
really an ocean of roses,
but I can't get back.

The light on his face
changing to dead,
and I can't get back.

Each second, the flicker
between re-scans of a screen,
and I can't get back.

*

Now that my ears are iffy
(*you* are?)
more and more
I hear doors slamming
through my feet,
trash rumbling off
through my feet,
stirring seeds,
fall coming, skitter in the walls,
through that airy
unscratchable spot
between my shoulders.

Off the top of my head
(higher than ears)
what you say
sounds dimmer than what you said,
sounds like
mail jammed in the slot,
a dog left long alone, the wind,
sounds like
the sun climbing a stone stair,
a stone's slow sigh in the sun.

Now that I can't hear
what you say, it means
so much, now that I don't hear
exactly, it can mean
anything, everything.
It means what I hoped.
It means what you hoped
it meant.

All of your secrets
I know, I know, but whose—
I've been in you
and out of you,
reading as you read, I've
been you.
I know everything,
but your name, your name, your name...

                    *

Remember the joke about lifers
(jokes, I didn't delete!)
who know the jokes by heart,
so they just say 12,
they just say 43
and get laughs. Well:

I just say 2, I say
3rd season of the year,
I say just 30 years, I say
that quirk of gladness
that's been in her face since she was 7,

without the run-up
of deleted fields,
the bird-crossed
deleted pain and wonder
as November twilight
deletes deletes deletes.

*

My great poems are: deleted.
What satisfaction, though,
to know they were written!
How magisterial
they must have been.
Faintly embarrassing their deleted
global sweep,
their wise but deleted
moan on behalf of all,
their poise delete delete
so much more automatic than my own.
Their great unanswerable last line,
You know what I mean!

So now the onset
of the final simplicity
that comes after great poems
which in anyone who hadn't
written such great poems
might just be senility!

With the mountainous
assurance of innocence
so rare in these late days,

with the mountainous freshness
of the first time,
I'll vouchsafe to Millions
that damburst of clichés
I've been saving up for decades!

That's what I'll DO!
That's what I'm doing!
They'll like me better,
I'll like them. I'll be happy
as all the other dumbfuck poets,
astonished and glad

to find that unexpectedly,
all that occurs to me—
every damn word—
is true. It's SO TRUE!!!

*

Now that I'm ready,
I get to be,
faster and faster,
the Posterity that forgets me!
O Reader, O Future
even you
are behind me!
Delete delete delete!

*

[Did you hear? It was Keats
and his gathering swallows.
He wrote that manic
Songs for Senility—
and him not 60—
and then and THEN...
it was SO ironic!]

Room Temperature

That coffee you forgot to drink,
this light, eight minutes from the sun,
words I thought for a second
the hottest ever written.

IV. Small Hours

Shore Town, Winter

Now that it's January
in Victorian New Jersey,
the aqua and magenta
gingerbread of triple-deckers
is past incongruous, way past forlorn,
and all the way to the Grand Canyon's
weird silence,

the loud absence
of the forces of improbable scale and precision
that must have made this
(and what a job to paint it!)
for their very own,
then flip-flopped down the boardwalk
and out of the galaxy,

leaving the sea,
pretty calm this evening,
the tide trending in,
the moon and sun, this winter twilight,
just about equally dim.

When Matthew Arnold settled one elegiac hand
on a pale shoulder, gesturing out
over the Channel, he saw France
quietly letting go its light.
This is America, we see nothing
but size, sky and ocean
working on gray-green
not much of anything,

though in this later century
we, also, hear the *grating roar,*
mixed maybe with a syringe or two
and indestructible packing, but never mind,
the hiss and click

of calciferous debris that Arnold heard
Sophocles hear as human misery.

Waves in themselves, turning to her
he whispered (and I whisper),
are huge but powerless.
Their megatons
collapsing on a single shell
leave it unfazed,
but hardness of touch, quickness of suspicion,
the quickening step
past pain:
shells break, we break, each other.
Ah love, etcetera.

Weary of detail,
Arnold's particular deity
has chilled out to think about the Big Picture,
and on his darkling plain
they've closed the stores,
as if in a day or two
his sun will go red giant
and scrape the planet down to the stone.

But the Sea of Faiths,
in the broadest sense, is doing
just fine, thank you. Endlessly it reproduces
Taco Bells and Jiffy Lubes
along our hardening arterials.
Not a day goes by
without the world recording
zillions of world records,
no day that our collective résumés
fail to add a zillion lines,
and those who declare
for Higher Things enrich
in desert compounds the uranium
of Zeal's white glare.

Over and over,
just when it seems we're blessedly
running out of gas,
idiot saints
figure out how to make money
from going on just as before.

Ah love, the news is old
that the wind slides through carless lots
and slaps flat on chainlink:
more than a century,
now, it's been the end of the world,
and this long, long twilight,
this last *Alas,* has lost its power
either to frighten or console.

On a similar shore
You and I are old, Ulysses crooned
but then again
'Tis not too late to seek a newer world.
We call it a day,
heading for Parkway North,
not too downcast to be lifted
by a car absurdly loud with teens
and a music that drowns ours
as they pass us, entering

this paused flick
of dark hotels and meters on Expired
hoping for solace and a Sign! a Sign!
and sure, if anything is sure, to find
both less and more than we have found
on a winter Sunday
in the flickering neon
of this new old new old world
that says *No Vacancy* and means
We are empty, and we plan to stay that way.

Tableau

Remember the one about the two intellectuals
walking the unwild woody trails
just out of sight of the houses? There among postsymbolic deer
unspooked by their conspicuous thrashing, they stumble
over rocks and branches, arms out, almost touching,
talking about, what else, poetry and their kids,
and wildly happy. The sky like a page
just turned to, your face just turned to me,
just that.
    The way things broken off
a little too soon can last forever.

Postmortem Georgic

If I die in June, the true end of our year,
exchange the storms for screens and summon the technician
to check the coolant pressure in the central air
before the dog days when the black drive wavers
and no bright metal can be touched, and then swap out the filters,
and now that our little grove of maple, oak and hickory
has shed into the gutters (oh deeper than you imagine)
petals and dust and unfelt leaves, flush them out
lest thunderheads that build in the searing afternoon,
toppling, leave them weeping around you.

Yes, if I die in summer you will be hard-pressed
to keep the shrubs clipped back and the grass down
till the heat browns it, and to counteract metastases
of chickweed, black medic and poison ivy.
Circle the house now with broad bands of pyrethrins
to dam the streams of carpenter ants, and if they keep coming
seek out their nests in stumps and the garden's railroad ties,
and kill them, if you have the heart (as I might not)
to battle life, having so little left of your own.

Trundle the recycling to the curb infallibly
on alternate Mondays, or if in weekless summer you forget
what day it is, do it any day and wait till it is taken
as all things are. Repair the small appliances that faltered
while you were drowned with work and could not bother,
or let them go, since little these days is worth repairing,
and service the car for journeys you have been putting off
that you cannot put off longer, now the world grows old,
or do not, and tell the world it must come to you.

But after all, I would never die in summer. Say to our children
as usual his mind has wandered, only this time so far
he has not come perfectly back, and then think the click,
a little too long, of setting your glass on the endtable

in the twilit air you cannot tell from your skin, is the click
of me also invisibly near you setting mine down.

If I die in autumn, exchange the screens for storms,
and set traps baited with nut butters
along the perimeter of the basement
and foam-caulk all exterior cracks and seams
to foil the mice, checking also the chimney cap
and the screening of the vents to keep out flying squirrels,
native to these woods, though many do not believe in them
with their huge black eyes all pupil, and their rustling above us,
and summon the servicer of the big hollow furnaces,
for when the cold like empty boxcars rumbles in
and the heat is creaking in the aluminum ducts
you will be cold, coldbones, without me,
listening awake to, what is it, the wind,
mysterious disk accesses, creatures flowing in the walls?

Turn the clocks back, slide fresh batteries into smoke detectors,
and reset the timed lights, for the days grow shorter
and you will be driving home in earlier and earlier sunset
and the day will hurt you with its unexpected darknesses,
like the young husband who could not speak his mind,
and now, before the year begins in earnest,
weed out your files, discarding a third of all you have
as the trees will, since leaves, also made for a single year,
grow shabby and slow, and heavy snows would collect in them
cracking limbs off and splitting even the thick trunk,
and travel light, for all you carry you will carry alone.

And when all the leaves are down, even the reluctant oaks,
blow them into the woods, or call someone to blow them,
and then, only then, scoop out the gutters
once again, lest they clog and freeze, sagging with ice-mass,
or call someone to do it. Then drain the mower and park it,
or sell it since you will not want to keep it up
or let the gas sour and the valves gum, since you will not sell it,
and think that of all seasons this is the one I would never miss,

and say to our children he is out for one of his long walks
and the leaves are streaming through his eyes and heart and hair.

If I die in winter, when there is little to do
but wait till winter is over, keep watch on the upstairs windows,
and if they ghost with mist, turn the humidifiers down
lest the paint peel and the sills rot out.
Restock the pantry with beans, onions, and root vegetables,
and the soups you love, salty and fat and thick,
for green leaves and the glare of fruits would hurt the soul
which wishes now to eat darkly and be deep in the ground.
Wind the hoses, draining them first, in coils,
squeeze clockwise the indoor shutoff
and open the outdoor faucets wide, letting the last water out
lest in a coldsnap some pipe snap.

Now broadcast salt preventively on the drive,
for it is steep, and mornings slick, and snow frequent,
or sleep in and wait till the sun has worked on it,
since in a few hours the sun will work on it,
or a few days or weeks, for what is time now,
and how can I urge them on you now, these endless tasks,
who am not sure in my own mind if they were life
or what kept me from our life. Then tell our children
I have gone to lie in the abstract earth,
breathing stones like sky, restless as always
to fit the huge, sharp planet into my too-small heart.

If I die in the spring, that fruitless season,
scour the markets for the grapes and nectarines
of the other hemisphere, for it is always harvest somewhere,
but stay wary through the middle of March
when wet, heavy snowstorms still may strike, only then
stowing the shovels and bringing out brooms and seeds.

Squeegee the windows till they squeak with clarity
and lime the lawn against sour rains, and if now, already,
carpenter ants are trailing over the sea-blue carpet

defenses have failed and they have nested in the house,
so listen in the walls for a noise like crackling cellophane—
I can tell you where, in the beams between floors
where the slow leak of the shower has spread dampness—
and drill there and spread fatal powders
or do not, since though they chew a house down,
they chew slowly, slowly, slowly and the house
will fall when it falls, and not before your fall.

Start the dehumidifier, lest books demoted to the basement
rot there, or let them, since those we will never read again,
set the clocks forward, and once more change the batteries
in the smoke detectors, or do not, and when the fire insurance
comes due in April, imagine, at least, that you might let it go,
for how in this late cold can we argue against fire?

Yes, if there is justice, though I have said there is none,
I will die in the spring, this season I love least
of beginning all over, I of no patience,
when hope is a door left unlatched in a high wind
banging and banging itself to pieces.

Now is, of all seasons, the season of paper,
and we have policies that make death a benefit:
you have lucked out, hit the jackpot, you are worth a million!
Now change your beneficiary and delete me from the mortgage.
Search out the bills in the right top drawer, and one drawer down
receipts organized in twenty-one categories
for the IRS—travel, supplies, books, charities, faiths, memories—
and burn them, paying no taxes, for this is the truth: you owe
nothing now, and were there a light *Judgment* burning in this night,
I would have come back somehow to warn you,
but there is no light, there is nothing, though you cannot believe it.

No, you will feel instead that I packed carefully,
taking everything that was ours, though I have nothing.
You will feel carjacked and pushed out on a curve,
watching the car you and I somehow are still driving

turn and stop and turn, until it has vanished
into the future we thought of, still happening without you,
though now, of all that could have been, there is nothing.
There is only where you are going, though you seem so still,
there is only that somehow we see each other
from two trains in the station, parting so slowly
we can't for the life of us say which of us is moving.

Night Lights

(1977-   )

A *shower, a cigarette?*
Slow of speech,
I answered with these decades when you asked
what I wanted next.

Blackout

Lights out, and gleeps of powerdown
in the middle of the shameful News.
You go to the window, hoping darkness
is Universal, and not just you.

The Rich Man Sotto Voce

Years I was poor but didn't have to be.
Months I was lost but knew the way home.
In my crazed minutes I took good notes.
Therefore, Lord, I do not complain.
Nor, lest you hear me and remember
how small my suffering, do I dare pray.

To a Tea

The way he asked it.
You were moved, unmoving,
the way a crowd
tightens at the exit.

Your eyes on him
slowly narrowed,
as if you were steadying to pour
into a cup the size of an atom.

Slice of Life

Instant before
pain's thunder, lightning:
the fingertip
crescent of blood
widening,
like someone you thought was asleep
rolling over and smiling.

Who Has Seen the Wind

The wind blows—nothing mostly—
blows its blowing—
happy to have what happens to be free
go where it's going.

Red, Green, Blue

Apparently I have no idea
what I've just said.
This plummeting elevator,
this choir
of silence holding one steep note:

I am the bomb squad poised above your heart
to snip... which tiny wire?

Star

Never and never again, song says,
love or pain like ours.
How vast a night one firefly
easily overpowers.

Reading Light

You look up from an oldish author:
Is he dead?
Such power we have,
not knowing. Let him live.

Roads Not Taken

It never came down to two roads at all,
or if it did, I took the one less traveled by
for a driveway, or the entrance to a mall,
or it slipped past like a station off the air
while I bent down to fiddle with the dial.

So many hours, so many guessed turns later,
I can't be sure the taillights I am following
are really the car I thought I was following.
One says *I know this road, we're really close,*
another *Uh, guys, we are totally lost.*

Actually we're having a pretty good time
singing and waving to singing and waving cars
that flare up head-on, fading to red behind us.
We don't have to be anywhere. The party we left
and the one we were headed to are probably over.

And as for those who might have been following me,
odds are I lost them long, long ago.
Nothing to do but keep on driving as clearly
as if I hadn't, flashing my change of lane and exit,
in case there's anyone who needs to know.

Roads Taken

Last bells of evening, toning *bronze*
and *bronze,* a hint of plaint.
Even if I hadn't heard the shuddering board,
the splash, the laughter, I'd have known
from the quaver of voices over water
that this is the last house in summer,
and now is the double loneliness
of missing a party you don't even want to be at.

The T'ang poet sets out on a thousand-mile journey,
minor administrative post in prospect,
chronic war rattling around the mountains
that might last all his life. And someone else
returns from a journey no one knows he's been on,
feeling again the thick air of the valley—
the children so tall—and whatever happens to love
that hasn't been used enough, has happened.
He spreads before them, as excuse or evidence,
what he has gathered, mottoes of gods and sages,
spells, strange weathers and archaic praises,
currency unfamiliar in this land.

End of Summer

Just an uncommon lull in the traffic
so you hear some guy in an apron, sleeves rolled up,
with his *brusque sweep brusque sweep* of the sidewalk,
and the slap-shut of a too-thin rental van,
and the *I told him no* a gust has snatched from a conversation
and brought to you, loud.
                    It would be so different
if any of these were missing is the feeling
you always have on the first day of autumn,
no, the first day you *think* of autumn, when somehow

the sun singling out high windows,
a waiter settling a billow of white cloth
with glasses and silver, and the sparrows
shattering to nowhere are the Summer
waving that here is where it turns
and will no longer be walking with you,

traveler, who now leave all of this behind,
carrying only what it has made of you.
Already the crowds seem darker and more hurried
and the slang grows stranger and stranger
and you do not understand what you love;
yet here, rounding a corner in mild sunset,
is the world again, wide-eyed as a child
holding up a toy even you can fix.
                            How light your step
down the narrowing avenue to the cross streets,
October, small November, barely legible December.

Notes

Section I in general: Most of the myths in these poems will be familiar. Persephone, Demeter, and Hades. Echo and Narcissus. Pygmalion the sculptor. Apollo and—is that Daphne? After he lost Eurydice, Orpheus was dismembered by the Maenads and his head floated down the river Hebrus, still singing. In the Iron Age (after the Golden, Silver, and Bronze Ages), Lycaon, king of Arcadia, served a meal of human flesh to Zeus, who turned him into a wolf. I've stolen the title of "Zeus: A Press Conference" from Adam Zagajewski's brilliant "Franz Schubert: A Press Conference."

"Metallurgy for Dummies": Tinnitus (TIN ih tus, by the way) is ringing in the ears.

"By the Numbers": Joke you don't have to get: *quarry* as in "a place you mine stone" comes from the same root as *four* and *square, quart* and *quarter*. But *quarry* as in "something you hunt" comes from a different root and is related to *cur* and French *coeur* (heart).

"Are We Alone? *or* Physics You Can Do at Home": This ramble has a few specific debts:

"The simplest and most popular cosmological model today…" —Max Tegmark, "Parallel Universes," *Scientific American,* May 2003, 41.

"Searches for extraterrestrial intelligence…" —Ian Crawford, "Where Are They?" *Scientific American,* July 2000, 39.

"How Much Does the Internet Weigh?" —Stephen Cass, *Discover,* June 2007, 43.

But more generally it riffs on dozens of other pop-sci articles (for which Brian Greene's *The Fabric of the Cosmos* would provide a teacherly and highly readable synthesis) and respectable but highly speculative ideas about multiple universes and other dimensions. Light from objects moving away from us (which is almost all of them) is shifted towards the red end of the spectrum. Objects approaching us are shifted towards blue. Yes, the earth's mass is indeed six sextillion tons and gravity is the weakest force, many orders of magnitude weaker, for example, than the electromagnetic force. According to last week's estimate ordinary matter and energy constitute 5% of the universe. Dark Matter (23%) and Dark Energy (72%), both so far undetected though they are presumed to be everywhere, make up the rest. Fact-checkers please note: I am the holder of a valid Poetic License from the New Jersey State Council on the Arts.

"Prokaryotes" are primitive cells, specifically bacteria with no nucleus and DNA not organized into chromosomes.

"The Stars in Order Of": "Soldiers and poor"—Edward Thomas, "The Owl." "Church-bells beyond the stars heard"—George Herbert, "Prayer." The Pleiades is a cluster of seven stars, though one is relatively faint and not everyone can see it (Tennyson couldn't). The constellation has some of these names in other cultures, but some of mine are made-up. On an 18th-century voyage to the Southern Hemisphere French astronomer Nicolas Louis de Lacaille named fourteen "new" constellations things like Telescope, Microscope, and Compass (not, however, Cell Phone). Readers of science magazines frequently come upon some version of the sentence "There are 100 billion neurons in the brain, about the same numbers as the stars in our galaxy." Very faint stars are best detected with peripheral vision, but we only see color looking head-on. Big Bang produced hydrogen and helium. Heavier elements up through iron were created by the fusion reactions in stars, elements heavier than iron in supernovas.

"Songs for Senility": Apologies to the shade of William Butler Yeats
    for filling a great passage of "A Dialogue of Self and Soul" with
    static. The real words are:

> What matter if I live it all once more?
> Endure that toil of growing up;
> The ignominy of boyhood; the distress
> Of boyhood changing into man;
> The unfinished man and his pain
> Brought face to face with his own clumsiness;
>
> The finished man among his enemies?

"Nine times the space that measures day and night" and "O how
fall'n! how chang'd"—*Paradise Lost*, Book I. "When such as I
cast out"—Yeats, "A Dialogue…" "The woods decay, the woods
decay and fall"—Tennyson, "Tithonus."

About the Author

James Richardson's books include *Interglacial: New and Selected Poems & Aphorisms,* which was a finalist for the National Book Critics Circle Award, the "cult favorite" *Vectors: Aphorisms and Ten-Second Essays, How Things Are, As If,* which was selected by Amy Clampitt for the National Poetry Series, *Second Guesses, Reservations,* and two critical studies. His poems, essays, and aphorisms have appeared in *American Poet, The American Poetry Review, Boulevard, The New Yorker, The Paris Review, Pleiades, Poetry, Science News, Slate, Yale Review,* and such anthologies as *Great American Prose Poems, Geary's Guide to the World's Great Aphorists,* the 2010 *Pushcart Prize,* and the 2001, 2005, 2009, and 2010 editions of *The Best American Poetry.* The recipient of an Award in Literature from the American Academy of Arts and Letters, the Robert H. Winner, Cecil Hemley, and Emily Dickinson Awards of the Poetry Society of America, and fellowships from the National Endowment for the Humanities and New Jersey State Council on the Arts, he has taught at the University of Virginia, Harvard, Princeton, and Columbia. For the past thirty years Richardson and the scholar-critic Constance W. Hassett have lived in New Jersey, never very far from their two brilliant daughters.

Since 1972, Copper Canyon Press has fostered the work of emerging, established, and world-renowned poets for an expanding audience. The Press thrives with the generous patronage of readers, writers, booksellers, librarians, teachers, students, and funders — everyone who shares the belief that poetry is vital to language and living.

Copper Canyon Press gratefully acknowledges board member

JIM WICKWIRE

in honor of his many years of service to poetry and independent publishing.

---

amazon.com®

Lannan

NATIONAL
ENDOWMENT
FOR THE ARTS

 WASHINGTON STATE
ARTS COMMISSION

Major support has been provided by:

Amazon.com

Anonymous

Beroz Ferrell & The Point, LLC

Golden Lasso, LLC

Lannan Foundation

Rhoady and Jeanne Marie Lee

National Endowment for the Arts

Cynthia Lovelace Sears and Frank Buxton

William and Ruth True

Washington State Arts Commission

Charles and Barbara Wright

*To learn more about underwriting
Copper Canyon Press titles, please call
360-385-4925 x103*

Lannan Literary Selections

For two decades Lannan Foundation has supported the
publication and distribution of exceptional literary works.
Copper Canyon Press gratefully acknowledges their support.

LANNAN LITERARY SELECTIONS 2010

Stephen Dobyns, *Winter's Journey*

Travis Nichols, *See Me Improving*

James Richardson, *By the Numbers*

John Taggart, *Is Music: Selected Poems*

Jean Valentine, *Break the Glass*

RECENT LANNAN LITERARY SELECTIONS
FROM COPPER CANYON PRESS

Michael Dickman, *The End of the West*

James Galvin, *As Is*

David Huerta, *Before Saying Any of the Great Words: Selected Poems,*
translated by Mark Schafer

Sarah Lindsay, *Twigs and Knucklebones*

Heather McHugh, *Upgraded to Serious*

W.S. Merwin, *Migration: New & Selected Poems*

Valzhyna Mort, *Factory of Tears,* translated by Franz Wright
and Elizabeth Oehlkers Wright

Taha Muhammad Ali, *So What: New & Selected Poems, 1971–2005,*
translated by Peter Cole, Yahya Hijazi, and Gabriel Levin

Lucia Perillo, *Inseminating the Elephant*

Ruth Stone, *In the Next Galaxy*

Connie Wanek, *On Speaking Terms*

C.D. Wright, *One Big Self: An Investigation*

For a complete list of Lannan Literary Selections from
Copper Canyon Press, please visit Partners on our Web site:

www.coppercanyonpress.org

The poems have been typeset in Sabon, an old-style serif typeface designed by the German-born typographer and designer Jan Tschichold (1902–1974) in the period 1964–1967. Headings are set in Gotham, a sans serif typeface by Hoefler & Frere-Jones. Book design and composition by Phil Kovacevich. Printed on archival-quality paper at McNaughton & Gunn, Inc.